Donated
in
Memory of

Alberta Bretey

Early Village Life

Bobbie Kalman

The Early Settler Life Series

Toronto
New York

Crabtree Publishing Company

To Caroline, our daughter, whose friendship we cherish

A very special thanks to Kathleen Scherf who
helped to research, design and edit this book.

I wish to also thank *Nancy Cook, Rosemary
McLernon, Trish Holman, Derek Western,
Sarah Peters, Phil Rodgers, Andrea Crabtree,
Stephanie Williams, Samantha Crabtree, Bill
Patterson, Barbara Snyder and Peter Logan.*

Copyright © 1981, 1989, 1991 Crabtree Publishing Company

Cover painting: New York Historical Association, Cooperstown

Cataloging in Publication Data

*Kalman, Bobbie, 1947 –
   Early village life*

*(Early settler life series)
Includes index.
ISBN 0-86505-009-0 hardcover
ISBN 0-86505-010-4 softcover*

*1. Villages   2. Frontier and pioneer life
I. Title. II. Series.*

HT 431. K 34   307. 7'2   C 81-094985-7

350 Fifth Ave, Suite 3308
New York, NY 10118

R.R. #4
360 York Road
Niagara-on-the-Lake, ON
Canada L0S 1J0

73 Lime Walk
Headington, Oxford 0X3 7A
United Kingdom

Contents

These backwoods settlers feel lonely for the friends and family they left behind. Today is Sunday, a day for rest, prayer and remembering. They read the Bible. There is not even a church nearby. Without a village, life was unbearable for many. As more settlers moved into an area and a village was born, the lives of these settlers changed for the better.

Before there was a village

Most of the people who came to North America two or three hundred years ago came here because they had to. Many emigrated for religious reasons, but most came because they were too poor to feed their families in the old country. When they arrived, some people went to work as servants for other farmers already settled here. Most of the earliest settlers had to start their new lives in the backwoods. Life in the middle of the wilderness was very

difficult. Often there was nothing more than thousands of trees. Many people felt homesick, lonely and discouraged about the future. They wondered whether they would ever have good times again.

A feeling of togetherness grows

Nonetheless, no matter how difficult life in the New World seemed to the new settlers, at least it offered the hope of a future. Their old country did not

Living alone in the woods was a sad experience for many. These settlers came from a European town. They were used to having a lot of friends. As soon as they have finished building a shelter and clearing the land around it, they will want to find out where their nearest neighbors live. When life is hard, people need the support of other people.

even offer that! People in Britain and Europe were without work. Families were starving! With new-found strength, the settlers in the New World got down to work to make better lives for themselves. They began to clear the forests, build houses and fences, and clear paths or roads for travel. When newcomers arrived, the more established settlers went out of their way to be helpful. They realized the hardships and loneliness these new people had to deal with, because they too had experienced it when they first arrived.

The native people in the area helped out the new settlers by teaching them how to raise beans and pumpkins. They taught the newcomers how to survive in the wilderness, how to hunt, and how to fish. The settlers learned how to make pottery, such as bowls and dishes. Later, the settlers bartered food and supplies for baskets, moccasins and beadwork made by the native people.

5

Growing food was one of the first and most important tasks for every pioneer. Without food, a family would not survive the coming winter. These ladies have done a hard day's work collecting carrots, turnips, onions, beans and potatoes from the fields.

Sharing their resources

The settlers realized that life was much easier if there were other people with whom they could share resources, work and good times. The earliest example of community spirit was seen in the borrowing system. People ran out of supplies because there were no stores in the area in which to buy them. Flour, medicine, soap and tools were commonly lent or borrowed. If one neighbor owned a hand quern, she would lend it to the other neighbors.

Bees buzz with peoplepower

Another important resource that was shared by the settlers was *peoplepower*. When a big job had to be done, such as the building of a barn, all the neighbors would gather and work at it until the job was finished. Many jobs were done in this fashion. These work sessions were called *bees*. Bees were very popular with the early settlers. They brought people together to help each other to do tasks that would have taken one family months to finish. Bees also provided good times for the settlers. Once the work was finished, people ate, talked and danced for hours. Young people met other young people at community bees. These gatherings led to romance and marriage for many.

Neighbors are helping one farmer to build fences to keep animals in. They have just had a logging bee. The neighbors helped cut down the trees in the field behind them so the farmer can plant a crop of wheat in it.

Trust thy neighbor

A feeling of community soon developed in an area. People believed in other people. No one ever locked their doors in the early days. People trusted their neighbors not to steal anything from them. If a traveler needed a place to sleep, he or she could just walk into a settler's home, find a place by the fire, and be gone before the family even woke up. It was a custom for the native people to leave the settlers some food if they stayed at a settler's home overnight. Most settlers welcomed travelers into their homes, as they too were welcomed by others when they had to travel.

Farmers, craftspeople, merchants and professionals

As more and more people moved into an area, there were always some who were not interested in farming. These settlers were either craftspeople, merchants or professionals. They could offer special services to the farming families in the community. These people were the pioneers of the early village.

Trees were everywhere. The settler's first house was made from the logs that were chopped down to make room for it. The ends of the logs were notched so that the logs would fit snugly together. The roof was made of carved out half-logs which were placed one row facing up and the next facing down in order to allow the rain to drain off.

The settler's first cabin was made of logs

When the pioneers arrived at their homestead, they first had to pick the spot for their home. Then they had to clear the land by chopping down enough trees for a cabin. The trees that were cut down to clear the land were used to build the log house. The logs were cut into the proper size by the settler. These newly cut logs had to have their corners notched so that the corners of the building would be more secure. The roof was made of hollowed out half-logs. The first row of these logs was placed hollow side up. The second row was placed hollow side down. One hollow log was placed in the middle of the two underneath it. In this way, the rain would run off the top of the log house and drain out from the bottom row of hollow logs. It would not drip into the cabin. The doors and windows were then cut out and the fireplace was built out of mud if there were no stones. The last step was to stuff all the cracks in the logs with mud, wood or moss in order to protect the family inside from the wind. The floor of the cabin was made of the packed-down dirt that was already there, or of planks cut from logs by the farmer.

A fireplace or stove was found in every log cabin. It provided heat for cooking and for warmth. This log cabin was an unusual one. It contained many ornaments. Most log cabins were bare except for a few pieces of furniture. What do you think of this settler's taste?

Inside the log house

Furnishings were usually simple. Sometimes colorful cushions were the only decoration. Braided rugs made from rags were on the floor. The whole family shared the one room for eating and sleeping.

The fireplace or stove was the central part of the loghouse. All the cooking was done there. It was also the source of heat on winter days. Since there were no matches in those days, the fire was never allowed to go out in winter or summer. It was too

difficult to start it again. People were forced to breathe the soot-filled air. The fireplace provided some of the light in the evening. Candles were also used. They were made from *tallow* (grease). Hot tallow was poured into a wooden mold and when it was cool, the candles could be lifted out by removing the top of the mold.

As the community became richer, the settlers helped each other to build wooden frame houses with two storeys. The log house then became the place to keep the animals. The settler's third house was usually quite large and comfortable.

This sheep is happy to be rid of its heavy wool. What was once its coat will now become the coat of an early settler. Sometimes this shearer was not as careful as he could have been. The end result was some pretty silly-looking sheep!

From sheep and flax to settler's slacks

The early settlers had to be self-sufficient. They came to their new homes bringing anything useful that they could carry because there was no place where they could buy new things. Even later, when a general store had opened up in the area, it was not always possible for people to get the clothes they wanted or needed. The settlers had to make most of their own clothes.

Wool and flax were the main ingredients for clothing. Wool came from sheep and was spun into winter clothing. Flax was a plant from which linen was made.

When sheep were ready to be shorn, they were first washed in the creek with a tobacco solution which killed the bugs that might have lived in the wool. The settlers would wait until the wool dried and then shear the sheep. The best wool was picked out and greased so that it would be easier to work with. The wool was then brushed with a *carder* which had two sets of teeth, one above the other. It came out straight and untangled. After the carding, the wool was spun into yarn on a spinning wheel and the yarn made into fabric on a weaving loom.

Flax was a plant grown by most of the settlers. It was pulled out of the ground and allowed to dry in the sun. The leaves were then pulled out. The seeds were beaten out and later pressed into linseed oil. The stems of the flax were soaked in water. After several days, the stems would split apart and the flexible middle part was taken out and pounded on a *brake*. The silky fibers were picked out and combed. This fiber was then spun into linen yarn.

After the wool was greased it was carded with a brush-like instrument. The carder removed the tangles from the wool.

The carded wool was spun into yarn on a spinning wheel and wound onto a spool.

Next, the yarn that was spun on a spinning wheel was woven into fabric on a loom. The fabric was then used to make clothes.

Quilts were made from small pieces of material sewn together piece by piece.

Rugs were braided out of shredded pieces of old rags. Everything useable was recycled by the pioneers.

The flax seeds are separated from the stems of flax on this rake–like instrument. The stems will then be softened and pounded on a brake. The soft inner fibers will be spun.

These silky fibers were separated from the outer shells and then combed. They are now ready to be spun and woven into linen material.

13

Settler self-sufficiency

All settlers raised animals for food and for trade. Chickens were kept for their eggs and meat. Cows provided milk for drinking and for making cheese and butter. Sheep provided the settlers with wool. Animals were often bartered for supplies from the general store.

Animal and vegetable fat was melted down into a hot liquid called **tallow**. *Pieces of twine were tied onto sticks and were dipped in the tallow, allowed to cool, and dipped again until the candles were the right thickness.*

14

After the grain was ground into flour in a hand quern, it was made into enough bread to last for several days. It was baked in an outdoor or indoor oven, depending on how hot it was outside. The settlers used outdoor kitchens or ovens in the summer.

Father bagged the turkey for dinner. Mother, Andrea and Stephanie prepared it for the oven. Stephanie fetched the logs from the woodshed and added a new one to the fire.

The settlers in the community worked together to raise the milldam. The gristmill would then be built on the shore. The rushing water from the pond turned the wheel, which then made the grinding stones turn. The stones ground the grain into flour.

The gristmill

When settlers chose a place to live, they usually chose a place that was close to a gristmill. Most settler families were able to grow their own food, make their own clothes, and trade with someone for the supplies they needed. However, without a gristmill, life was very difficult.

Some people owned a quern or a mortar and pestle, but grinding one's own grain by these methods was slow and tiring. People would rather walk long distances, carrying their grain on their backs, in order to have it ground by a miller.

Once the settlers grew more grain than they would themselves use, they could trade it for other goods. The miller, together with the storekeeper and the owner of the sawmill, kept track of what was traded by the settlers. Instead of using money, people traded goods for

other goods or services. The owners of the gristmill, the sawmill and the general store were the most important starters of the early village. It was their services that attracted more settlers into the community. The new settlers then offered other services to the people already there.

Until there was a miller, it was difficult for a community to exist. As soon as a village started to grow, somebody would be found to fill the job. Perhaps one of the new settlers was a miller back in the old country. If there was no one in the community who knew how to run a gristmill, the position of miller was advertised in the nearest town. Once a miller was found, the whole community worked together to build the mill, and the new village was off to a good start. As soon as the mill was there, others opened new businesses in that area.

16

Before there was a gristmill, the settlers had to grind their grain by hand using a mortar and pestle. It could take hours to grind enough for a loaf of bread.

Some of the settlers owned hand querns. The grain was poured through the hole into the middle of the two stones which ground it into flour.

The miller's son weighs the flour that was ground from farmer Wilson's grain.

Once the settler had sacks of flour on hand, baking bread was no longer a big job.

The general store provided the settlers with foods and products that they could not make in their own homes. Coffee and tea were sold there. A giant coffee grinder was used to grind the beans into the powder from which coffee was brewed.

The store made the settler's life a lot easier. Farmers could now buy different kinds of groceries and produce there instead of having to grow them. They could trade one item for another. The store operated on the barter system. The storekeeper was like a banker. He or she kept track of what everyone traded, owed or had credit for.

The general store

The general store was a most important part of the early village. Before the store opened its doors, people had to travel from farm to farm lending, borrowing and trading supplies. Trading without using money was called the *barter system*. People decided between them how much various items were worth. Then they traded the items. The general store made the barter system work even better. All the farmers could now bring produce to the store and trade it there for supplies. The storekeeper decided on the value of each trade. The storekeeper also provided the community with supplies from the city.

Goods and services under one roof

The general store provided much more than supplies to the people who lived

nearby. It was a place where people could meet to solve community problems. A potbelly stove in the center of the store was a cosy place for people to gather to discuss problems, good news, or community plans. The general store in the area was also the community business center. Deals were made there, services were set up, and people were brought in touch with other people who had similar needs. In most cases, the general store was also the post office. Mail was dropped off and collected there once a week. The store was the social gathering place in the community. The family of the storekeeper went out of its way to make it cosy for the customers. Often hot bread and fresh cheese followed by steaming coffee or tea awaited people who traveled long distances to trade at the store.

A huge pile of logs is hauled to the river by two hard-working horses. The teamster sits on top. He could be crushed if the logs shifted and fell off the sled. The logs will be floated down the river to the sawmill in the spring.

The sawyer is sawing planks with a muley saw. It moved up and down to cut the log. It was replaced by the round, rotary saw.

The sawmill

The first settlers in a new area had to cut down trees to clear fields for farming. There were many ways to use the trees which were cut down. The settlers used the big round logs to make a log cabin. But making buildings out of huge logs was hard slow work. The settlers needed planks that were lighter and easier to work with. They began cutting the logs into planks with whipsaws. One person stood on a platform above the log, while another person stood below the log. It took a long time to whipsaw one plank.

Planks were needed to build many things in the village. Farmers needed planks to build a plank house. A plank house could be larger than a log house and it was much easier to build. The farmer also needed planks to build all the buildings needed on a farm, such as a barn, a chicken coop, and an ash house for smoking meat.

The houses of the minister, the doctor and the gristmill owner needed to be built with planks. The gristmill and the general store needed planks. The craftspeople of the village needed planks. Planks could be made much more quickly in a sawmill than by two people using a whipsaw.

To cut all the planks that were needed in the village, someone would build a sawmill. The sawmill was built beside a river. The river was dammed up to make a millpond just above the sawmill. The sawyer (the man who sawed the wood) allowed water to run from the millpond against the mill's waterwheel. The rushing water turned the waterwheel. The turning waterwheel turned the saw which cut the wood.

The sawyer needed many, many trees for cutting. After all the trees had been cut down around the sawmill, the sawmill owner paid the farmers in his area to go deep into the woods to cut logs in the winter. The farmers floated the logs down the river to the sawmill in the spring. Then they went back to their farms to plant their seeds.

These frozen children are happy that their teacher had the schoolhouse warmed up by the time they arrived. They had to walk an hour through chilly winter winds. They huddle together near the stove trying to warm their frostbitten little fingers and toes.

The village school opens its doors

In the early days it was not easy for parents to send their children to school. They had to get together, build a school, hire a teacher and pay the teacher's wages, as well as buy any school materials that were needed. The amount each family paid depended on how many children there were in that family. In those days people did not pay with money. They paid with work, food or supplies. They traded or bartered goods or services for other goods and services. Some of the villagers built the schoolhouse, some boarded the teacher at their homes for part of the year and others supplied clothing or school supplies. If there was a teacher before there was a school, lessons would be given in someone's home, in the general store, or in the village church.

Children learned *reading, writing and arithmetic* in school. They were taught Christian values, but they did not learn about any one religion.

The schoolhouse was usually a simple log cabin with a big box stove in the middle and two or three rows of benches and tables. Students had to supply their own slates, paper and ink. In the winter the ink would freeze on the way to school. The quickest way to melt the frozen ink was to leave it on the stove. Sometimes students would leave the cork in the ink bottle on purpose. As the ink melted, the pressure in the bottle would build up and the cork would pop out with a loud *bang*. Even then children played tricks on their teachers to rattle their nerves!

Before the church was built in the village, the schoolhouse was often used for Sunday church services. The visiting preacher reads a passage from the Bible to the congregation.

Children of all ages were taught by the same teacher in one room. These little ones wonder whether they will ever know enough to be able to divide those numbers.

Amy and Frank are having trouble with their arithmetic homework. They put their heads together and try different ways to figure out the problem on the slate.

23

Sally Hanson goes a-dancin'

The school provided a center for social events in the community. The settlers, especially the younger ones, loved the events because they were a break from the daily work of pioneer life. These events gave people a chance to relax and to get to know others in the community.

Sally Hanson, one of the young ladies who attended the village school of Middleboro, had looked forward to the coming dance for weeks. In all the excitement, she never thought about the fact that she did not have a dress to wear. Just a few days before the dance, Sally heard some of the older girls talking about the new dresses the village dressmaker was sewing for them.

Sally went home crying that night. It just was not possible for her to have a new dress. There was no time to have one made. She simply could not go to the dance!

Mrs. Hanson learned about her daughter's heartbreak from her younger daughter, Melissa, who was all too willing to make fun of her sister. Mrs. Hanson thought hard about Sally's problem. The day before the dance, she asked Sally to come straight home after school.

When Sally walked in, there, hanging on the door, was one of the prettiest blue gowns she had ever seen. She couldn't believe her eyes! Blue was her favorite color. It matched her eyes and brought out the shiny streaks of her long blonde hair. She could not figure out how her mother could buy her such a beautiful dress in such a short time! She would surely be the prettiest girl at the dance!

Mrs. Hanson admired Sally in her new dress. She explained that she had been saving her wedding gown for Sally. Since it was so important for Sally to go to this dance, she dyed the gown blue with some indigo she got from the general store. Sally met her future husband at the dance that night!

Sally models her new dress for the dance.

Sally met Charles Stell, her future husband, at the school dance. This picture was taken years later, just before they got married.

Sam Walker was the village schoolteacher. He lived with the Hansons. He was just a few years older than Sally. He too thought she looked attractive at the dance.

Mrs. Hanson is proud to have come to Sally's rescue with her wedding dress.

Teaching was more than a job

The district schoolteacher was respected by all in his or her teaching role, as well as in private life. Teachers had total control over what children were taught at school. A district teacher taught children of all ages in one classroom. Sometimes teachers were almost as young as their students. A person did not have to have a lot of education to become a teacher.

Most teachers lived with one or more families in the district during the school year. A teacher who boarded with a family was thought to be the smartest person in that household. People would ask the teacher's advice on decisions that had to be made. The teacher wrote the business letters for the family, read the paper to the old, and looked after the sick.

Churches of different denominations were usually the first public buildings to be built in a village. People traveled far to attend services at the church of their choice and to meet their friends there for a chat afterwards. Courting often took place after church was over.

26

The community becomes a congregation

At the time of the early settlers, there were few churches built. If a group of settlers had a school or a general store, sometimes church services were held there. Sometimes people traveled to the nearest towns or villages to attend Sunday services. Often families would spend a whole day visiting with friends until it was time for the evening service, after which they traveled home. The preachers gave morning service in their own parish church, rode on a rough road and held noon service at a community schoolhouse, and then rode to another settlement. After all that, they still had to travel home.

Circuit preachers

In the west, where there were fewer people and the communities were more spread out, circuit preachers traveled great distances to spread the word of God. Many circuit preachers covered areas that were over three hundred kilometres square. They conducted services, marriages, presided at funerals and preached against sin. Because of the size of the area they had to cover, the jobs were never-ending. Only the most dedicated people became circuit preachers.

Called upon by God

Sometimes the pioneer preachers were not really educated or ordained clergymen, but anyone who felt called upon by the Lord to lecture for Him. The settlers didn't mind this. To them the service was just as meaningful.

The village churches are built

After an area was settled enough to call itself a village, churches were the first public buildings to be built. There were usually at least two churches in each village. Religion was a very important part of early settler life.

Richard Nolley was a dedicated circuit preacher. No matter what the odds against him were, he always kept going. If his horse died, he walked. His dedication lasted throughout his lifetime. He died on his way to a Sunday service at a remote community.

This country doctor traveled an hour by horse to reach his sick patient. He tries to give her some tonic. The patient's family looks sad and worried. In those days doctors knew very little about what caused diseases, so fighting them was a difficult task!

28

Doctors did not receive patients in an office as they do today. They made house calls. They carried the medicines they needed in their bags and gave them to their patients on the spot. Often the doctor was also the apothecary.

Doctors or health hazards?

Doctors emigrated from Europe and Britain. Their passages were paid for by their services on board ship. Doctors had to bring most of their medical supplies with them, as it was difficult to buy them in the New World.

The doctors in those days knew little about diseases or how to cure them. Two of the most popular remedies used by doctors were bleeding and amputation. When a patient suffered from an illness it was believed that the best cure was to get rid of some of his or her blood. Small cuts were made in the skin and the blood was allowed to flow out until the doctor felt the disease was gone. However, the strength of the patient also left. Often people were too weak to recover from a "bleeding".

Amputation was the cutting off of a diseased arm or leg. Doctors knew nothing about sterilizing their instruments, so often they infected the limb even more by amputating a part of it.

Doctors also recommended that patients lie unwashed in dark, stuffy rooms while they were sick. Fresh air and water were believed to be harmful to a sick person.

Home healers

Most villages had only one doctor. Sometimes there was only one doctor for two or three villages. Doctors traveled to their patients. Often, however, it took a long time for a doctor to arrive. The settlers started practicing medicine on their own. For example, if they had a headache, they would chew the bark of the willow tree. Settlers also bought tonics at the general store. The tonics promised to cure everything from pneumonia to upset stomachs.

Bartering a cure

Doctors were not paid in money. A settler would pay a doctor in food, supplies, or services. A broken leg might have cost two chickens, the birth of a baby perhaps a hammer from the general store, and an amputation might have meant a service from the amputee's family, such as the mending of a broken fence.

The printer is removing the printed pages of the flyer. It tells people about a steamer excursion. It will be posted in the general store, gristmill and blacksmith shop, as well as on the outsides of buildings in the village.

Printing the village news

The printer printed newspapers, religious pamphlets, almanacs, schoolbooks, medical handbooks and government papers. Today printing is done with advanced cameras which are able to reproduce print and artwork exactly.

In the early days, printing was a long process. Each of the letters that were used in a word were handmade out of metal. These letters were called *matrixes*. Matrixes were stored in a wooden frame called a *composition*. The composition housed trays of letters of various type sizes and styles. Words were set up in

composition sticks about 5 cm long. The words were transferred to the galley from the composition sticks. The *stoneman* decided what the page would look like in finished form and laid out the type and pictures in that way. The stoneman then framed the page with an iron frame and drove wedges in between the frame and the galley so that the matrixes would stay in place when the galley was lifted. The finished galley was then placed into the press machine. Ink was spread over it. When a piece of paper was placed on top of the inked galley, the result was a printed page.

The printer shows how a block of metal into which a picture of a steamboat was etched will produce a printed picture.

From inked galley to printed page, the posters are now finished. The printer will have them distributed to the villagers.

Printers also printed books. When the pages were finished, a bookbinder bound them together by hand. Colorful endpapers dry on the lines above. The bookbinder moves the ink around in the tray to get the swirling effect of colors on the endpapers.

Bad road conditions meant a lot of new and repaired horseshoes. The blacksmith always had work to do. His trusty companion, Sam the dog, kept the other animals in line.

The village blacksmith also fixed farmers' tools and made other useful articles of iron for the home. The young boy, above, has brought in his broken hoop for repair.

The blacksmith helps animals and people

When people in a community decided that they had enough work for various craftspeople, they talked to the people who might be interested in doing the jobs. The settlers promised to help put up the buildings in which the craftspeople would work. Once a village started to form, more immigrants moved into the area. Instead of just working on farms, immigrants could work at the crafts in which they had been trained in Europe. They could start their own businesses.

The blacksmith was one of the most important craftspeople in the community. The blacksmith shop was always located in an easy-to-reach spot, usually at the main crossroads of the community. When farmers could not work on their crops, such as on rainy days, they would gather up all the tools that needed to

be fixed and go over to the blacksmith shop. The blacksmith shop was another social center in the village. There were posters on the walls announcing upcoming events, such as auctions, dances and bees. There was usually a newspaper at the blacksmith shop. One could catch up on the latest news while having a horse shod.

The blacksmith shop was usually quite noisy. There were always people sitting around talking and laughing. The banging of the hammers never stopped. Because blacksmiths worked with animals so much, people often thought of them as veterinarians. Farmers asked their advice on how to cure sick animals. Blacksmiths were sometimes even asked to pull people's teeth.

While the blacksmith was busy repairing the farmers' tools, the farmers exchanged village news. One of them even brought his fiddle along to help while away the time.

The blacksmith shop was a busy place

The blacksmith made horseshoes and oxshoes and nailed them to the hoofs of the animals. Blacksmiths also made hinges, latches, spits for the fireplace, farm tools, nails, locks, logging chains, hoes, rakes, axes, hammers and spades. They used charcoal to heat the iron they worked with. The blacksmith's apprentice had the job of keeping the fires hot enough to melt the iron.

Gigantic bellows were used to blow air on the fire to keep it hot. Often a whole bull hide was used to make one of these huge bellows. The blacksmith either used a mold to make an object, or the object was hammered into shape on the anvil. The anvil rested on the butt of a log near the *forge* or fireplace.

34

The pewterer made objects of pewter. Pewter dishes, teapots, candlesticks and mugs were used by the settlers. Pewter was cheaper than silver. It did not break, so it was more economical to use than earthenware or china. The pewterer took the pewter metal, which was a combination of tin and lead, melted it down, and then put it into molds. When the object came out of the mold it was sanded and polished. The picture, above left, shows the pewterer polishing one of the goblets that was later placed on the shelf (above right).

More metalworkers set up shop

The silversmith was a little like a banker. When a settler had a lot of silver coins and didn't want them lying around the house, he or she had them melted down by the silversmith. Today, when we have saved enough money, sometimes we buy gold or bonds with it. In those days there were few banks, so people had their small silver coins or small silver objects melted down and made into one larger silver object. When a settler had a teapot made from coins, the teapot was worth the same amount as the coins had been. Silver was valued according to its weight, not its shape. It was important that the settlers trusted their silversmith not to steal some of the silver and replace it with a cheaper metal, such as copper. All of the settler's wealth was in the hands of the silversmith. Silversmiths often joined clubs and led civic activities in order to gain the trust of the settlers.

The silversmith prepares a coil of silver to be flattened as he pulls it through the press. He will then make bracelets from it.

The cooper, above, planes a branch on one side to make a hoop for one of his barrels.

The cooper made barrels, buckets and tubs of all types and sizes.

Barrels, buckets and tubs

The cooper was a barrel-maker. In the early days there were no plastic and styrofoam cartons or plastic jugs in which to keep food or supplies. Almost everything was kept in barrels. Eggs were packed in barrels of oatmeal to prevent them from breaking. Liquids of all kinds were also kept in watertight barrels. The cooper was one of the busiest craftspeople because barrels and buckets were used every day to hold hundreds of items.

In order to make a barrel, the cooper bought planks from the sawmill. The planks were shaped perfectly so that they would make a tight fit when pulled together. The cooper made the tops and bottoms of the planks narrower. The middle of the planks was the widest point. This caused the barrel shape. The cooper stood the planks upright with a temporary

wooden hoop holding the planks together at the bottom. A cord was wrapped around the top of the barrel, pulling the planks inward. Wooden hoops were then put around the top, middle and bottom of the barrel.

Wooden covers were placed in the circular openings at both ends. The top could be pulled off on dry goods barrels. For watertight barrels a round hole was cut in the top. The liquid was poured into the barrel through this opening. Another round hole was cut in the side near the bottom. A spigot or tap was placed in this hole. When the tap was turned on, the liquid poured out.

Tubs and buckets were made the same way as big barrels, except that the planks were narrower at the bottom so that the tops would flare out.

The wheelwright above hammers a mortise into the hub of the wheel. The tenons of the spokes fit into the mortises so tightly that it was almost impossible to pull them loose. Wheelwrights not only made and fixed wagon wheels. They made all types of wheels and repaired them as well. The wheelwright below repairs a mill wheel.

The village on wheels

Wheelwrights worked closely together with the wainwrights, who were the wagon-makers. The wheelwright's job was to make wagon wheels. First wheelwrights made the wooden hub of the wheel, a circular block of wood. Into this they cut holes called *mortises* around the rim of the hub. One mortise was cut for each spoke. A *tenon* on the end of the spoke fit into the mortise. A wagonwheel usually had fourteen spokes. The tenons were made to fit exactly so that the wheelwright merely had to tap them in and they would not come loose again. The circular rim of the wheel was made up of curved wooden *fellies*. Each felly had holes cut into it for the other ends of the spokes. The spokes went all the way through the hole in the felly. The wheelwright measured the spokes so exactly,

that they did not come through the other side of the hole. The entire rim was then covered by an iron *strake*. The strake fit very tightly because it was first heated, then fitted, and then cooled down quickly by cold water so that it shrank to make a tight fit.

Shoes could not be bought in the variety of colors and sizes that we buy them in today. They were made to order. The cobbler was the craftsperson who made and fixed shoes.

The dishes, bowls and jugs have been shaped, glazed and fired. The potters stand by to take the pottery out of the kiln. One of the potters admires her handiwork.

Other craftspeople offer their services

The potters

Most of the first dishes and bowls used by the early settlers were made from clay. Potters dug up the clay and mixed it with water to clean it. The heavy impurities sank to the bottom, while the vegetable matter floated on top. The clay was mixed with sand to prevent it from cracking when dried. It was then kneaded, shaped either by hand or on a wheel, and baked in a hot kiln for twenty-five hours.

The cobblers

In the early days most jobs required people to stand or walk all day long. New shoes were always needed by the settlers. The cobbler repaired, as well as made new shoes. Both shoes were made exactly the same, so that they could be worn on either the left or the right foot. The upper part of the shoes were hand sewn. Sometimes the soles were also sewn, but most often, the uppers were nailed onto the soles by wooden pegs. Cobblers often made other articles of leather as well, such as mugs, saddles and harnesses.

The joiners

If there was not a sawmill in the area, the joiners were the craftspeople who planed down planks to a certain size. The main job of the joiner, however, was to finish off the interior woodwork of a plank house. Joiners made stairways, cupboards, paneling and simple furniture. The joiner and the cabinetmaker did most of the woodwork inside a house. A joiner was a carpenter. Sometimes the joiner was also the cabinetmaker. Sometimes the sawmill owner made the articles that the joiner made. As the village grew into a town there was enough work for all three craftspeople.

Inns and taverns provided a place for tired travelers to rest. Stagecoach drivers stopped at inns to have their horses changed for new ones. Inns always had stables for weary and hungry horses, as well as beds and food for tired people.

Inns and taverns for travel and relaxation

Inns and taverns were built for two reasons. For travelers they provided a place to stay, food to eat and people to talk to on long, lonely journeys. For the community dwellers, the inn was a place to go for drinks and entertainment. In the early inns the furniture was very simple. The main room had tables and benches in it. The kitchen had a large fireplace or stove around which all the utensils were placed. There were different types of bedrooms. Those who had more money could afford to sleep in beds with sheets on them. Even in the better rooms one could not be assured of privacy. One usually paid for a sleeping place. That meant that three more people might be sleeping in the same room.

People not only had to share their beds with other people, they also had lice and bedbugs as company. At many inns there were rooms in which there were no beds or furniture. One had to lie on the floor on straw mattresses without sheets. There were no bathrooms in those days either. The guests washed in a log trough. People could also rent rooms at the inn for business deals. Traveling salespeople could meet there with the village merchants. The village barber, who was often also the dentist, had a chair in one of the rooms of the inn. People could come to have their hair cut and teeth pulled at the same time. Market day was a busy day for the innkeeper. People came in to the taverns for a drink and to wait for friends there. Then they would travel home in groups.

The smaller inns and ordinaries were most likely to have a wash closet somewhere behind the house instead of a bathroom inside the house. Guests shared the water bucket, the pan and one towel. One could also wash some clothes in the large bucket on the floor.

The ordinary grows into an inn

Inns and taverns usually appeared in villages after the gristmill, sawmill and general store were already there. The inn often took over as the village social center. School meetings, social events, auctions and club dinners were held there. Small villages usually could not support an inn. Sometimes farmers were given money to operate an *ordinary* in their home. They provided a meal and a bed for travelers, and food for horses. If many travelers used the ordinary, it grew into an inn before long.

Mr. and Mrs. Rodgers set up an **ordinary** in their home. Mrs. Rodgers prepares breakfast for her traveling guests.

Both young and old alike looked forward to maple sugar time in the bush. Nothing in the world tasted as delicious as fresh maple sugar hardened on pure white snow!

Working together meant fun

When the community was still spread out people would walk long distances to visit neighbors. Sometimes they would just sit around and smoke, play cards, or talk. More often than not, however, the pioneers took part in some kind of organized activity. Many of the activities centered around work. After the work was done, there was plenty of food, dancing and fun. These work-parties were called *bees*.

From sap to taffy

In February or March sap started to run in the maple trees. Maple sugar time was both a busy and a romantic time in the bush. There was a lot of work to do. Holes were bored into the trees, wooden spouts were driven in and buckets were hung under the spouts. The sap ran into

the buckets. Sometimes the sap ran so fast that a person could barely empty a bucket into the large central vat and carry it back to the tree before the next bucket was full to the rim with sap. The sap was boiled down in the vat into a thick syrup.

Young people loved to take part in maple sugar time. It gave them a chance to meet other young people in the community. It allowed them to romp happily in the bush. But best of all, they got to make the syrup into wonderful - tasting maple taffy. They looked forward to the taste of the freshly cooled taffy. The syrup was poured into the pure white snow. The snow caused the syrup to harden and become candy. This way of making candy was called "sugaring-off". Both the experience of being outdoors and the taste of the maple sugar were just too good to pass up.

The whole community turned out for this barn-raising. The men are erecting the frame. The ladies pose in their party dresses. They have prepared a feast to be eaten in the newly built barn. A square dance will follow.

Piling up the logs

The object of the logging bee was to clear the farmer's land of trees. All the settlers in the neighborhood were invited with their axes and oxen. The logs were piled up by the farmers and dragged by the oxen to wherever the settler wanted the piles to be. The driver of the oxen, together with four or five other workers, stacked the logs in a pile. The trees that were not needed were burned on the spot. If there was a big area to be cleared, logging teams would compete against each other to see who could finish their part first. The prize was usually a jug of whiskey. After the chores were finished, a big party was held until the wee hours of the morning.

The barn goes up

Settlers went to raising bees to help neighbors build wooden houses or barns. Sometimes for a larger building, as many as one hundred people helped out. The farmer prepared for the raising bee by having the logs cut, notched and numbered. The farmer also laid the foundation. Only the planks had to be put up and nailed on. If the bee was properly organized, the building could go up in a matter of hours. A big party followed in the newly built house or barn. Because the settlers cooperated so much, they managed to build community buildings, such as schools, churches and shops in a very short time. Everyone looked forward to the work, the fun and the future use of the new buildings.

The girl in the middle of the picture cut off her peel in one piece. She drops the peel on the ground. The letter it forms will be the first letter of her future husband's name.

The apple bee

Because the settlers could not buy their applesauce or juice in cans, as we are able to, they had to preserve their apples for the winter. In the fall it was necessary to core and pare the apples before they could be made into cider or applesauce. It was common to invite neighbors and supply a plentiful lunch after the paring. After the lunch, there was a party.

There were always games at apple bees. In a favorite game, settlers tried to peel off the skin of an apple in one piece. The peel was then thrown up into the air and allowed to land on the ground. When it fell, everyone would gather to see what letter the peel resembled. The letter was supposed to be the first letter of the name of the parer's future husband or wife.

Quilting together

Women young and old, married and single, gathered at the quilting hostess' house and helped to sew quilts for her household. In the early evening the men came and everyone sat down to a tasty dinner. They drank tea and ate biscuits, toast, cakes, preserves and sweetmeats. When the meal was over everybody would join in games, conversation and laughter until the day ended.

Husking corn

In the fall, stalks of corn were piled high on one side of a settler's barn. People came over around six or seven o'clock and spent the evening husking corn. The husked corn was piled on the opposite side of the barn. Tin lanterns lit up the barn when it got dark. The huskers stopped work around ten and had a dinner and dance in the barn. Sometimes, however, the party started as soon as the huskers arrived. Judging from the pictures of some of the bees, it was hard to believe that any work was done at all!

This old picture appeared in an 1858 newspaper. These young people are at a corn-husking bee. They seem to be having a lot of fun! The girls on the right try to put cornsilk into the young man's hair. His girlfriend is not pleased about all the attention he is getting!

Quilts were made by groups of ladies, young and old. They were joined by their families for a party in the evening.

The people, above, have had a busy day cutting down stalks of corn. After the work, they enjoy a late corn-roast.

On November 5 each year, British settlers celebrated "Guy Fawkes Day". They burned effigies of Guy Fawkes, who tried unsuccessfully to blow up the British parliament buildings in 1605. The effigies were at first made of turnips, as they had been in England. The settlers, however, discovered that pumpkins carved into scary faces were much more frightening. Guy Fawkes Day is no longer celebrated in North America. Pumpkins are now carved into jack-o'-lanterns on Halloween.

Mr. Perry is happily showing off the blue ribbon their cow won at the fair. Sarah, his daughter, knew Betsy could win all along! She rewards Betsy with some sweet hay.

The fall was a time for hard work, fairs, pumpkins and celebrations

The fall was one of the busiest times for the pioneer community. The crops had to be harvested. The wheat stalks had to be cut down, bundled and threshed. The wheat grain was taken to the grist mill to be ground into flour. Corn had to be picked and husked. Apples and other fruit were collected and preserves were made. Vegetables were put away for the winter. Produce was taken to pay off debts at the general store. The whole village and farming community worked together to finish all the tasks before the snow fell. And, in the midst of all this work, there were fairs to visit, pumpkin effigies to make, and Thanksgiving to celebrate. When all the work was done, people partied their way right into the Christmas season.

While these girls work hard harvesting the wheat, they think about the barn dance that will take place tonight. ➤

*After Thanksgiving dinner these children challenged their father to bob for apples.
So far it looks as if he has come up with nothing but a very wet face!*

48

Blindman's bluff was one of the favorite parlor games played both at Thanksgiving and Christmas. The person who is "it" has to touch and identify the person caught.

"Harvest Home" becomes Thanksgiving

Thanksgiving was also known as "Harvest Home". It was not always celebrated on the same day every year. It took place when all the work of preparing for the winter was complete. These fall celebrations were held to thank God for the good harvest. The church and the homes in the community were decorated with some of the fruit and vegetables which had been gathered.

The celebrations began with a gathering of people in someone's home. Then, while the men went hunting, the women would prepare a feast and the children would play outside.

Later, there was a community dinner of beans, meat pies, fruit pies, squash, turnips, pickles and salads, as well as turkey. After the dinner, people talked, played parlor games, dunked for apples or went out for walks. It was a day of happiness for the whole community.

Some people attended church on Thanksgiving day. These settlers watch the clock. The parson has made his sermon too long. The community dinner at the schoolhouse has already begun. The settlers are anxious to get away.

Valentine's day was an important day for courting. Young men sent romantic letters or cards to young ladies in the community. The country postman was busy delivering messages of love to ladies of all ages. The little girl in the picture also expects to receive a letter.

Barnaby considers himself a good catch, but he is surprised that Mabel decided to do it with a hook. Mabel, on the other hand, would prefer the fish that got away!

This sleigh of wedding guests seems to be winning the race back to the bride's house. The ladies wave to the friends left behind. Will the driver get to kiss the bride? If not, he certainly will have his pick of ladies to kiss right there in his sleigh!

Love settler style

When a young man showed interest in a young lady, courting began. The man started to spend his evenings at the home of the young lady. Her father decided if he was a welcome guest or not. Sunday was also a popular day for courting or *sparking*. Couples often met each other on the steps of the church. The man then escorted the lady home.

Weddings were a community event

In the early days wedding invitations were either made in person, or sometimes not at all. When a couple in a community decided to get married, the rest of the community was naturally expected to be there. Everyone looked forward to weddings because they usually meant days of partying.

Weddings often took a long time to arrange. There were not a lot of ministers in the neighborhood. Couples sometimes had to travel quite a distance to get married. The ride to the church was usually a race. It was a wonder that so many people managed to get married with all the races that took place. It was not unusual to find the bride, groom and half the guests sprawled all over the road after their sleighs had overturned. However, people always managed to make it back to the home of the bride after the wedding. The first male guest to arrive got to kiss the bride!

Every year on Christmas Eve in this village a pantomime play was put on in the school-house by the settlers. Mother and Grandmother prepare the costumes, while Dad goes over the actions he has to perform in the play. The baby has fallen asleep in his arms.

Old Christmas celebrations

When settlers first arrived at their homesteads, they worked day and night building their new home, pulling up stumps, planting crops, and raising farm animals. In the first year, there was little time to celebrate anything, even Christmas. Work was the only pastime. However, once a pioneer family was well settled and a community was born, there was plenty of time for fun, especially in winter. Christmas was the biggest winter celebration. People worked hard all fall just to prepare for it.

The Christmases celebrated in the early part of the nineteenth century were

fun for the adults. There were parties before and after Christmas. The holiday season lasted almost three months. Some of the favorite Christmas activities were tobogganing, snowshoeing, skating and sleighing. Indoors, there were dances, parties, parlor games, pantomimes and concerts.

The villagers got together and put on pantomime plays. Sometimes these were staged indoors at the village school. Sometimes costumed actors performed in the streets or from house to house. This house to house play was called *mumming*. It often got out of hand, as

Birdie and Bijou hope that while they sleep Santa will bring them the dolls, toys and candy they ask for in their letter. Santa found their note. They will be happy children in the morning! Santa left them each a baby doll, some candy canes and a wooden sled.

the mummers were offered drinks at each house.

Children did not enjoy Christmas as much in those days. There was usually a church service and a huge Christmas meal with a plum pudding on Christmas Day, but there were few or no gifts. Although the settlers decorated their homes, no one, except a few German settlers, put up Christmas trees. There was little about this old-style Christmas for children to enjoy.

New Christmas customs

Christmas after 1850 became more like the Christmas that we now celebrate.

The Christmas tree appeared as the symbol of Christmas celebrations. The newspapers all started to print stories and pictures of a new Christmas figure called *Santa Claus*. No one knew what Santa looked like. Some of the papers showed him as tall and thin, others as small, round and fat. Thomas Nast, a cartoonist, finally drew a Santa that everyone liked. He was jolly, short and stout, and wore a red suit. After Santa became popular, gift-giving also started as an important Christmas custom. Store-bought gifts replaced home-made ones in most households. Children received many presents, as they do today.

Snowshoeing into the bush was a new and welcome activity for the settlers. One could see groups of young people on snowshoes heading in to explore the woods.

Skating was one of the most popular outdoor winter sports. The settlers flocked to frozen ponds and lakes for a day of fresh air, exercise and socializing.

Winters lured the villagers outdoors

Even the smallest settlers loved a good snowball fight!

When a settler talked about his or her family, it usually meant a husband or wife, children and parents or in-laws. The grandparents played a big part in helping to raise the grandchildren. In the picture above, a grandfather educates his granddaughter about the family history. A stroll through the village cemetery was a good way to begin learning about the family tree. The family Bible was another good source of information for finding out about those who lived before. Have you ever searched into your roots?

Sometimes settlers lived too far away from a school and the children had no way of getting there. The grandparents helped to teach the children how to read and write. Often the parents were too busy or tired to do it. There really wasn't much time for "book learning", as both the grandparents and children also had a lot of chores to do. However, while mother cooked and father worked in the fields, the grandparents were the most likely people to find the time to read to the children.

Beth's grandfather tunes up for the Christmas service at the village church. Beth loves to hear him play his violin. Someday she hopes to play as well as he does. He has begun to give her lessons. Beth is happy to have Grandfather living with her. She can spend as much time as she wants to with him. They enjoy many of the same things in life.

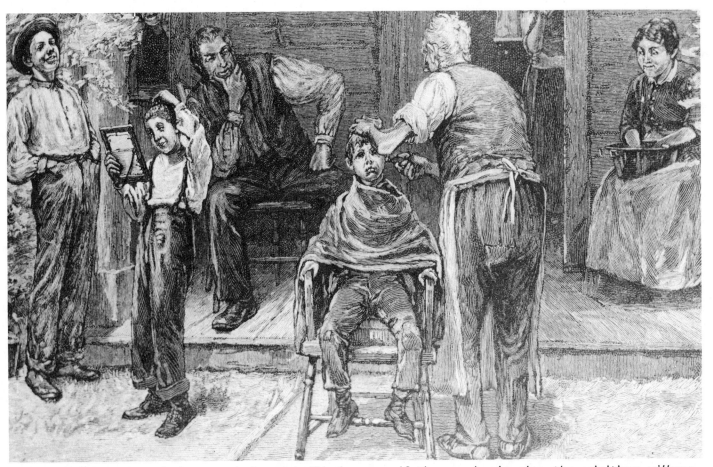

These boys admire their new haircuts. Their grandfather, who is also the visiting village barber, has done a fine job. They are lucky that they don't have to pay for their haircuts.

Grandparents helped to raise the children

Most of the settlers lived by the Bible. Ruth reads a passage to her grandfather. They read the Bible together every day.

Sometimes being with one's grandmother was not as much fun as being with one's friends! However, Tom and his dog do their duty without complaint.

Little adults

After children were past the toddler stage, their clothes were made to look like small-sized adult clothes. When children were as young as five, they were also expected to do small-sized adult chores. There was little time for play in the early settler household. Children woke up early, had a bite to eat, and started right off doing their chores. They collected the eggs, milked the cows, fed the animals and picked berries in the bush. The children who lived in the village, such as the children of the storekeeper, did chores in the store for their parents. If there was a lot of work to be done, parents took their children out of school for as long as it was necessary to get the job at hand finished.

This little pioneer was sent to bring the geese in from pasture. She has tried to round them up several times, but they will not budge. They have attacked one of the pigs and are determined to fight to the finish. Susie weeps because she is missing her dinner while they fight. She dare not go home without them. It will soon be dark.

These children have been in the fields all day picking huckleberries. It was one of the jobs they enjoyed most. They got to run, talk, sing and play in the sunshine. The best part, however, was eating the delicious huckleberry pies for supper.

The first chore Henry and Peter had to do in the morning was to fetch water from the nearby river. Carrying the heavy bucket was a back-breaking job. However, in winter, they were able to use their little sledge to pull the full bucket back home.

In pioneer days, cheese, butter and bread were made in the home. A new cheese factory meant settlers could now buy cheese.

Instead of baking bread for hours each week, the pioneer could buy fresh bread daily from the bakery.

Alison dreams of owning a dress shop in town. She does not enjoy working on the farm. She wants to be a businesswoman.

Villages grow into towns and cities

As more people moved into the community, more services were offered. New merchants, craftspeople and professionals set up businesses. As more businesses opened, more settlers moved into the village or into the area. Life was easier when there were other people to do jobs, such as sawing logs into planks, grinding grain into flour, making clothes and furniture. Settlers were attracted by the businesses, and the businesses provided new jobs for the settlers. As railroads were built through the villages, the villages grew into towns almost overnight. It was easier for people and goods to move from one place to another. Young people were no longer happy working on farms. They dreamed of starting their own businesses in town. Villages did not stay villages for long. Towns and cities grew quickly in their place. Factories replaced workshops and department stores replaced small merchants.

Glossary

accommodation *a place providing rest and food for a traveler*

almanac *a book that lists all kinds of facts for a certain year*

amputation *the cutting off of a diseased limb of the body*

anvil *the block of heavy metal on which the blacksmith works*

apothecary *a druggist*

axle *a rod that runs under a carriage connecting two opposite wheels so that they will turn at the same time*

backwoods *heavily wooded, thinly settled area*

barter system *the exchange of goods without the use of money*

bee *a merry gathering of people working together*

bellows *an air pump operated by scissor-like handles*

brake *an instrument used to crush flax or similar plants*

carder *a brush-like instrument with upper and lower teeth used to untangle and straighten out unruly fibers*

circuit preacher *a minister who traveled around on regular routes preaching the word of God*

community *a group of people living in the same area, under the same government, sharing resources, public buildings, roads and interests*

composition stick *a small, hollow wooden stick about two inches long, in which matrixes were placed to form words before being placed into the galley for printing*

congregation *a group of people who band together for religious worship*

courting *when a young man and woman are getting to know each other romantically; dating*

craftspeople *people who make their living practicing hand crafts, e.g. cooper*

diplomat *an expert in dealing with people in difficult situations*

effigy *the image or likeness of a public figure*

emigrant *a person who leaves his or her country forever*

flax *a blue-flowered plant from which a fiber is extracted to make linen cloth*

forge *the big open fireplace in the blacksmith's shop*

foundation *the sturdy basement of a building, usually constructed from brick or stone*

galley *the container which holds the matrixes from which, when inked, a page of print is made*

game *hunted animals*

hand quern *a hand-turned grain mill made of two stone wheels, one on top of the other*

hide *the skin and fur which has been stripped off a dead animal*

homestead *a farmer's house, outbuildings and land*

husk *the outer layer of corn which is peeled off*

immigrant *a person who comes to a new country to make it his or her home*

indigo *a very dark blue color made from the indigo plant*

linseed oil *an oil made from pressing the seeds of the flax plant*

loom *an instrument used to weave yarn into fabric*

matrix *a metal plate used in printing on which a letter or picture is carved*

merchant *a storekeeper*

moccasin *a leather shoe with beads and fringes, made by the native people*

mortar and pestle *a device made up of a bowl-like container and small crushing-stick used to grind up small amounts of various material such as medicines*

notch *a small cut out of an object, usually made so that it could be fitted properly to another object.*

ointment *a pasty mixture applied to heal a wound*

ordinary *what a house was called when the owners were paid to allow travellers to rest there*

pamphlet *a small, soft-cover magazine, usually about one particular subject.*

professional *a person who holds a job for which some higher education is needed*

remedy *something that relieves or cures a sickness*

resources *a natural wealth that is commonly shared, such as forests*

slate *a small chalkboard on which early settler students did their work*

solder *to join metal together*

spigot *a wooden faucet*

stoneman *the person responsible for completing the galley in printing*

tallow *a substance used in making candles, made by boiling down fat*

tonic *a liquid, drinkable medication*

trough *a very long, narrow box filled with water*

wilderness *unsettled, uncultivated land*

Index

Acknowledgements

Library of Congress, Dover Archives, The City of St. Augustine (FSNB), Colonial Williamsburg, Scugog Shores Museum,
Port Perry, Century Village, Lang, The Peterborough Post Card Company, Upper Canada Village, Black Creek Pioneer
Village, Ministry of Industry and Tourism, Metropolitan Toronto Library, John Ross Robertson Collection (T 15866),
The Public Archives of Canada, Harper's Weekly, Canadian Illustrated News, Frank Leslie's Illustrated Magazine, Bobbie
Kalman, Peter Crabtree, Ontario Archives.

1112131415 LB Printed in the U.S.A. 9876543